THE CHRISTIAN INSTITUTE

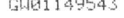

The Fourth Commandment

RUPERT BENTLEY-TAYLOR

Copyright © The Christian Institute 2023

The author has asserted his right under Section 77 of the Copyright, Designs & Patents Act 1988 to be identified as the author of this work.

Printed in May 2023

ISBN 9-781901-086669

Published by:
The Christian Institute, Wilberforce House, 4 Park Road, Gosforth Business Park, Newcastle upon Tyne, NE12 8DG

All rights reserved

No part of this publication may be reproduced, or stored in a retrieval system, or transmitted, in any form or by any means, mechanical, electronic, photocopying, recording or otherwise, without the prior permission of The Christian Institute.

All scripture quotations, unless otherwise indicated, are taken from the HOLY BIBLE, NEW INTERNATIONAL VERSION®. NIV®. Copyright © 1973, 1978, 1984 by International Bible Society. Used by permission of Zondervan. All rights reserved.

The Christian Institute is a Company Limited by Guarantee, registered in England as a charity. Company No. 263 4440, Charity No. 100 4774. A charity registered in Scotland. Charity No. SC039220

Contents

5   1. Introduction

11   2. The Biblical evidence

25   3. Six words

29   Bibliography

31   References

1. Introduction

Up to about fifty years ago, a high view of the Lord's Day, as the outworking of the Sabbath principle for the New Testament believer, was standard among English-speaking evangelicals. The list of those who wrote and spoke strongly about observing the Lord's Day or the Christian Sabbath sounds like a roll call of the 'greats' in evangelical history. Without attempting to be exhaustive, the list includes the Puritans such as Richard Baxter, John Owen, Matthew Henry, John Bunyan and the authors of the Westminster Confession of Faith, as well as John Wesley, George Whitefield, Jonathan Edwards, Robert Murray M'Cheyne, Charles Simeon, Henry Martyn, DL Moody, Charles Hodge, JC Ryle, Charles Spurgeon, Gerhardus Vos, Martyn Lloyd-Jones, George Duncan, William Still, James Philip, John Murray, JI Packer and more recently David Searle, Alistair Begg and Kevin DeYoung.

Of course, generations of Christian leaders and teachers could be quite wrong. But in the face of such a consensus, and the evident godliness and scholarship represented in the list above, a measure of humility about any variant judgement is in order. At least, we would do well to examine the issues carefully before concluding that fresh light has come to us which was denied to them.

But today, I know leading evangelical preachers and pastors, whom I love in the Lord, and Gospel-preaching churches I respect, that dismiss the relevance of the fourth commandment with little hesitation. Among the younger generation of Christians, there are many to whom the whole notion of one day set aside for God seems a quaint throw-back to Victorian values. In fact, they would not be inclined to read a booklet like this, because they would consider it such a non-issue as to be hardly worthy of discussion.

It is easy to feel intimidated by the tide of this popular thinking within the evangelical world. I was once advised to think very carefully about writing about the Lord's Day, because I would bring upon myself such a storm of criticism. It is argued that previous generations of Christians made Sunday observance a heavy burden and merely reflected the culture of those times. But the argument cuts both ways. There has been a broad cultural shift in our society. The significant degree to which legislation and society's attitudes supported keeping Sunday special is now only a fading memory. The timing of the shift in evangelical thinking about the place of Sunday could be construed to look suspiciously like an accommodation to the prevailing winds in society.

Here are three reasons to give this special attention:

1) The very fact that the fourth commandment is part of the Ten Commandments gives it special importance

When Jesus handled aspects of the Ten Commandments, such as 'Do not murder' and 'Do not commit adultery', far from watering down the commands, he applied them more deeply. His handling of those commands act as a paradigm for us. Jesus indicated that each individual command highlighted a whole area of concern to God, and of importance for mankind. It would be surpassingly strange if there was nothing of significance for mankind as a whole in any one of the Ten Commandments, declared by the voice of God, and written by the finger of God on stone. That includes the fourth.

2) Dismissing the relevance of the fourth commandment has a kind of avalanche effect on one's whole understanding of the Ten Commandments

In 1982 Don Carson contributed to and edited a book entitled *From Sabbath To Lord's Day*.[1] The authors reject the view that the Sabbath was a creation ordinance, and argue that the fourth commandment was a part of the ceremonial law, not the moral law. Still, the book also argues for the continuing relevance of the Lord's Day for the New Testament believer, but detached from any Sabbath principle. This book was widely read and has had significant effect in shifting the thinking of many about the Sabbath.

If the fourth commandment can be shown to be irrelevant for a believer today, it no longer makes any sense to speak of the Ten Commandments having an abiding authority as a summary of God's moral law. As Douglas Moo says,

> *I am arguing that the Sabbath commandment is a crucial 'test case', suggesting that the Ten Commandments, in their Mosaic form, were not intended by God to be eternally binding on all people everywhere.*[2]

In that case, we presumably should remove the words of the Ten Commandments set up on the walls of churches all over our land. The consequences of taking this position can be pressed in very far-reaching ways. To be fair to Carson, while he detaches the Lord's Day from being based on any creation Sabbath principle, he personally maintains a special place for the Lord's Day, and would not treat the day in a manner much different from those who do root it in Genesis 2. Nor would he dismiss the relevance of the other commandments, because he regards them as validated in the New Testament. However, as a highly respected scholar, his influence spreads far and wide and many others are much more radical in applying this sort of thinking.

Yet I do not wish to overstate the rejection of the fourth commandment. There have continued to be books arguing the case for the abiding significance of the Lord's Day, such as those by Brian Edwards[3] and Joseph Pipa[4]. Indeed, it seems to me that in the last decade there has been something of a fresh reassertion of its value. One thinks of weighty scholars such as John Frame[5] and Greg Beale,[6] and widely influential writers and preachers, with their slightly different nuances, such as John Piper and Kevin DeYoung,[7] and some of the material from the Jubilee Centre in Cambridge.

All of these argue for the special place the Lord's Day should have.

3) The fourth commandment has profound significance for whole communities, since it benefits society as a whole

This is why The Christian Institute has consistently resisted legislative moves to extend Sunday trading. It is not just an individual matter. To have a designated day of rest prospers individual *and* family life. Some people accept the idea of having a day off, but argue it does not matter which day an individual takes. This view reflects a typically Western individualism that is a world away from either the Old Testament or the New Testament. The day of rest is not just a break from work for *me*, but a break in which I can invest in the most significant relationships of life, in my immediate family and among my friends. And of course, it is also very significant for church life and gathering. But it also benefits the whole population when there is a recognised and regular rest from work. That is why it is so alarming that the Jubilee Centre leaflet, published in 2015, reports:

> *More than one in five households has at least one parent who regularly works both weekend days... Over a quarter of businesses require their employees to work on Sunday.*[8]

What is at stake here is not some abstruse theological argument, but the welfare of our society. Over the years there have been significant voices in the trade union movement and the business community that have recognised the value for our society of a day set aside. There is more to life than buying, earning, and working, and many non-Christians recognise that. We do not have to insist on a particular stance on exactly how the Lord's Day should be respected in an individual's life, or take a position on each debated point. But the underlying issue is one that affects our whole society.

Even so, the issues raised by the fourth commandment are complex. Don Carson, in his editor's introduction to his book, wrote:

> *It is one of the most difficult areas in the study of the relationship between the Testaments, and in the history of the development of doctrine.*[9]

John Frame identifies six views of Sabbath observance simply among Reformed theologians.[10] After reviewing Paul's comments relating to the Sabbath, and arguing in essentially the same way as I am about to, Frame comments, "I don't see any argument that will put the debate completely to rest."[11] Online you can find an ocean of comment easy to drown in. In the scope of what I am covering here, I will not explore all dimensions of the topic, but I wish to give serious consideration to the biblical evidence for the abiding significance of the fourth commandment.

2. The Biblical Evidence

1) The notion of the Sabbath is rooted in creation, and therefore has a claim on all human beings

In Genesis 2:2-3 we find this statement:

> *By the seventh day God had finished the work he had been doing; so on the seventh day he rested from all his work. Then God blessed the seventh day and made it holy, because on it he rested from all the work of creating that he had done.*

It is an interesting fact that God, who could have created the world in one day, or a hundred, chose to create it in six days, and rested on the seventh day which he "blessed" and "made holy". Some have argued this is simply to do with God and has no implications for human beings. I, for one, find that difficult to credit. To quote Frame:

> *it is hard to understand why God would have structured his work in a six-plus-one pattern if not as a model for creatures... It seems obvious to me that God intended the six-plus-one pattern for man's edification and imitation.*[12]

John Piper says:

> **The week exists.** *That is not to be taken for granted. Days exist because that is how long it takes the earth to rotate. Months exist because that's how long it takes the moon to wax and wane. Years exist because that's how long it takes for the earth to revolve around the sun. But why do weeks exist? They do not correspond to any phenomenon in nature. The answer is: the week exists because of Genesis 2:2... God worked six days and rested on the seventh. That set the pattern of the week.*[13]

The attempts made after both the French revolution of 1789 and the Russian revolution of 1917 to set up ten-day weeks totally failed, because somehow God seems to have written into humanity a seven-day cycle. Thus, previous to the giving of the Law in Exodus 20, the Israelites were to recognise, in regard to their collection of manna, "a day of rest, a holy Sabbath to the Lord" (Exodus 16:23). Just as Cain knew that he should not murder, in Genesis 4, and Joseph knew that adultery was totally wrong, in Genesis 39, both well before the Law was given, so Israel had a prior sense of a special day in the week. Thus when we get to Exodus 20:8, the fourth commandment is introduced with the words "Remember the Sabbath day by keeping it holy." It was not a novel notion. And Exodus 20:11 specifies that it was grounded in the events of creation:

> *For in six days the LORD made the heavens and the earth, the sea, and all that is in them, but he rested on the seventh day. Therefore the LORD blessed the Sabbath day and made it holy.*

In the Old Testament Law the application of the fourth commandment extended to aliens, servants and animals:

> *On it you shall not do any work, neither you, nor your son or daughter, nor your manservant or maid servant, nor your ox, your donkey or any of your animals, nor the alien within your gates, so that your manservant and maidservant may rest, as you do. (Deuteronomy 5:14)*

There is a fundamental necessity of weekly physical rest, both for animals and human beings. This feature can hardly be construed as merely part of the era of the Mosaic Law. Rather it is an abiding necessity.

At this fundamental level even those who dismiss the relevance of the fourth commandment have to recognise its abiding functional significance. So Thomas Schreiner, who argues that "we have no indication that the Lord's Day functioned as a fulfilment of the

Sabbath… the Sabbath has passed away now that Christ has come", adds, to my mind somewhat awkwardly, "It is wise naturally for believers to rest, and hence one principle that could be derived from the Sabbath is that believers should regularly rest. But the New Testament does not specify when that rest should take place".[14] Similarly another scholar, Wayne Strickland, writes:

> *The worship of God on Sunday is not in any way fulfillment of the Sabbath command… However the principle of Sabbath rest is established as a wise course of action.*[15]

2) The Sabbath had special significance for Israel

In Deuteronomy 5, the fourth commandment is presented in a slightly different way from the reasoning in Exodus 20. It is connected with commemorating the Exodus from Egypt:

> *Remember that you were slaves in Egypt and that the LORD your God brought you out of there with a mighty hand and an outstretched arm. Therefore the LORD your God has commanded you to observe the Sabbath day. (Deuteronomy 5:15)*

In Exodus 31:14-17, the Sabbath is described as a lasting covenant. "It will be a sign between me and the Israelites for ever." Beyond being a creation pattern, the Sabbath therefore had a special function for Israel to commemorate both the history of their redemption, and as a sign of the covenant. In the Old Testament Law the Sabbath was to be taken very seriously: no work was to be done on the Sabbath and no fires were to be lit (Exodus 35:3). Indeed, so seriously was it taken that to break the Sabbath law was to result in the death penalty (Exodus 31:14-17, 35:2), though whether this was ever carried out beyond the occasion described in Numbers 15:32-36 is not clear.

The Sabbath principle also extended in other directions. Every seventh year, debts were to be cancelled (Deuteronomy 15:1-11) and the land was to be left uncultivated, having "a Sabbath of rest, a Sabbath to the LORD" (Leviticus 25:4). The Year of Jubilee was after "seven Sabbaths of years" (Leviticus 25:8-55), when land reverted to its original inheritors and debts were cancelled. As one Bible dictionary puts it "Sabbath legislation, it may be said, is integral and essential to the basic laws of the Old Testament and the Pentateuch."[16]

Now these aspects of the Old Testament Law are part of what has passed away in the New Testament era, with the coming of Christ. Jesus observed the Jewish Sabbath as part of his perfect obedience to all that the Law required. However, the New Testament church, which initially met every day (Acts 2:46), did not simply continue meeting on the Jewish Sabbath. The Judaisers, who troubled the New Testament churches, tried to impose on the new Gentile believers circumcision, and keeping of the details of the Mosaic law such as the observance of Jewish food laws and festivals, including Jewish Sabbath observance. Paul, however, strongly resisted them (Colossians 2:16-17, Galatians 4:9-11). Calvin says on this topic:

> *When we hear that the Sabbath was abrogated by the coming of Christ, we must distinguish between what belongs to the perpetual government of human life, and what properly belongs to ancient figures, the use of which was abolished when the truth was fulfilled... So far as the Sabbath was a figure of rest, I say, it was but for a season; but inasmuch as it was commanded to men from the beginning that they might employ themselves in the worship of God, it is right that it should continue to the end of the world.*[17]

Some distinction must be made with each of the Ten Commandments concerning ways they applied in the Old Testament era which are not binding today. Few would dispute the abiding relevance of the prohibition of adultery (the seventh commandment), for instance, but we do not, as New Testament believers, apply stoning for adultery as commanded in Leviticus 28:10. Jesus himself did not in John 8, though he commanded the adulteress to leave her life of sin, so he is not disputing her guilt.[18] In the same way, when Paul called for action against a man who committed incest in 1 Corinthians 5, he did not call for his death, as Leviticus 18:29 had commanded in the Old Testament Law, but rather expulsion from the church until he repented. In each case, there is a principle that abides, even when the application is different in the New Testament. It is the same with the fourth commandment.

3) Jesus' teaching

Some people speak as if the New Testament were silent about the fourth commandment. It is said to be the one commandment not reiterated by being quoted in the New Testament. However, none of the first three of the Ten Commandments are quoted verbatim in the New Testament either. Yet it would be completely wrong to say they are not dealt with.

Jesus, while fully observing what God commanded in Old Testament Law regarding the Sabbath, was often at loggerheads with the restrictive and narrow understanding of the Pharisees concerning Sabbath observance. As John Piper says:

> *Jesus did not come to abolish the Sabbath but to dig it out from under the mountain of legalistic sediment and give it to us again as a blessing rather than a burden.*[19]

In Mark 2:27-28, Jesus makes a most significant statement:

> *Then he said to them, "The Sabbath was made for man, not man for the Sabbath. So the Son of Man is Lord even of the Sabbath."*

"The Sabbath was made for man." The word "made" is significant. It is not the ordinary word for "made"; it can be translated "was created". It is exactly the word used in John 1:3, "Through him

[Christ] all things were made," and again in v.10, "the world was made though him." In other words, the very word associates the Sabbath with creation, echoing Genesis 1 and 2. As Frame says, "Jesus in this verse finds the origin of the Sabbath in creation, rather than in God's covenant with Israel."[20] Jesus goes on, "the Sabbath was made/created *for man*." The word *man* is the general Greek word for mankind, ἄνθρωπος. The Sabbath is not made for Israelites, but for the human race – for our benefit. That fits everything we have already considered in our earlier section.

Don Carson challenges this, saying, "the word 'man' is used neither to limit the reference to Jews, nor to extend it to all mankind; that question is not considered."[21] But he recognises that this is a minority opinion: "the number of writers who reason thus [that is, that the Sabbath was made for all mankind] is staggering."[22] That could just be because this is much the most obvious inference: mankind is in view.

Jesus was very clear about the passing away of the Old Testament sacrificial system and temple worship in Jerusalem. He was direct in declaring all foods clean, and asserting that in Him all the Old Testament promises and types found fulfilment. He quite often disputed with the Pharisees about their understanding of the Sabbath; but he did not declare the principle redundant. Schreiner acknowledges: "Strictly speaking, Jesus does not clearly abolish the Sabbath",[23] and Moo says, "He (Jesus) does not clearly teach the abrogation of the Sabbath command".[24] One can only agree.

4) The apostolic practice

It is one of the most extraordinary features of the New Testament Church that it began to meet on another day of the week than the Jewish Sabbath day. This break with the seventh day was deliberate and revolutionary. The indicators of this practice are few but significant and consistent. In Acts 20:7, Luke records that in Troas, "On the first day of the week we came together to break bread."

Luke's language implies that this was a regular habit. 1 Corinthians 16:1-2 also indicates a pattern of setting aside money "on the first day of the week". This is almost certainly linked to their gathering on that day, as it was designed to remove the need for a collection when Paul came.

The words "on the first day of the week", in Acts 20:7 and in 1 Corinthians 16, are a translation of a very unusual Greek phrase. Piper says:

> *Literally it would read, "the number one of the Sabbath." That is, "the day which is number one in the sequence of days determined by the Sabbath" (Jewett, The Lord's Day, p. 75). Words for "first" occur over 150 times in the New Testament. And only in reference to the day of the resurrection do we get this unusual usage.*

Piper adds that the same phrase is found just four times elsewhere in the New Testament, all in reference to the day of Jesus' resurrection in Matthew 28:1, Mark 16:2, Luke 24:1, and John 20:1. He goes on:

> *The point is that the Christian church made the change from the seventh to the first day for worship because it was the day that the Lord Jesus rose from the dead.*

In Revelation 1:10, John says, "On the Lord's Day I was in the Spirit." John Piper comments:

> *John does not call one day in the week "the Lord's Day" as one option among many. He calls it "the Lord's Day" because he and the early church treat it in a special way among all days.*[25]

There is an almost overwhelming consensus that the Lord's Day was a reference to Sunday, the resurrection day. The term, the Lord's Day, is unusual in that it is not a normal genitive, but an adjectival phrase, which is only found elsewhere in the New Testament in the term the Lord's Supper. Just as the Lord's Supper *looks back* to

Calvary in the past, is a regular reminder of it in the *present*, and looks forward to the future messianic banquet in glory, so likewise the Lord's Day *looks back* to the resurrection, is a regular reminder of it in the present, and looks forward to a final *future* fulfilment in eternal rest in glory ahead.

This practice of God's people meeting on Sunday represents a shift from the Old Testament Sabbath day on Saturday, yet is rooted in the same principle of the Sabbath we can trace back to Genesis 2. I find it very strange that numbers of notable scholars argue that the Lord's Day is a completely different thing from 'the Sabbath' and has absolutely no connection to the fourth commandment at all. It seems to me that the Lord's Day is manifestly based on that commandment. Jesus went to the synagogue Sabbath day after Sabbath day. We go to church, Sunday after Sunday. What that represents, and what He was doing and what we are doing, are clearly on the same trajectory. Normal labours are set aside that day, worshippers come together, the Scriptures are read, the Word is explained, prayers and praise are offered, and fellowship enjoyed, in both eras. The New Testament has never been some wholly new thing completely disconnected from the Old Testament. It is not floating free. The apostles' practice and teaching are rooted in the revelation of God begun in Genesis and climaxed in Christ.

5) The teaching of Paul

Now here we come to the nub of how many justify their view that the fourth commandment is redundant. Paul wrote in Romans 14:5:

> *One man considers one day more sacred than another; another man considers every day alike. Each one should be fully convinced in his own mind. He who regards one day as special does so to the Lord.*

Again, in Galatians 4:9-11:

> *But now that you know God – or rather are known by God – how is it that you are turning back to those weak and miserable principles? Do you wish to be enslaved by them all over again? You are observing special days and months and seasons and years! I fear for you, that somehow I have wasted my efforts on you.*

And in Colossians 2:16-17:

> *Therefore do not let anyone judge you by what you eat or drink, or with regard to a religious festival, a New Moon celebration or a Sabbath day. These are a shadow of the things that were to come; the reality, however, is found in Christ.*

In the light of these passages, the debate is over for some; the Sabbath principle is manifestly redundant. We should not, however, proceed with such haste but rather look again more closely at what Paul wrote.

Observe firstly that neither of the first two passages refers to the Sabbath at all by name. Romans 14:5:

> *One man considers one day more sacred than another; another man considers every day alike. Each one should be fully convinced in his own mind. He who regards one day as special does so to the Lord.*

This passage is introduced by the command that the stronger brother should accept the man whose faith is weaker without condemning him, whether the point of dispute was over food or treating certain days as special. Romans 14:4:

> *Who are you to judge someone else's servant? To his own master he stands or falls. And he will stand, for the Lord is able to make him stand.*

Paul uses the example of those who considered some days more sacred. There is no doubt that this would most naturally refer to those converted Jews who still wanted to observe Old Testament festival days and the Jewish Sabbath day, though the details are not specified. But is this a reference also to Sunday observance as a special day, which can be said to be rooted in a creation principle? If it is, are we to understand that the apostle John must be classed as among those weak in faith because he thinks of one day as "the Lord's Day" (Revelation 1:10)? Surely not. I do not think John's attitude to the Lord's Day fits very comfortably with this understanding of Romans 14. Even Moo, who does not believe in the abiding relevance of the Ten Commandments, agrees that here in Romans 14:5 the "reference to early Christian observance of the Lord's Day… is almost certainly not present."[26]

Next let us look again at Galatians 4:9-11:

> *But now that you know God – or rather are known by God – how is it that you are turning back to those weak and miserable principles? Do you wish to be enslaved by them all over again? You are observing special days and months and seasons and years! I fear for you, that somehow I have wasted my efforts on you.*

It seems clear that Paul is referring here to a whole mindset that saw observation of special days, months and seasons as a path to spiritual life, gaining some sort of merit. Paul may have in mind observing Pagan festivals again, or those Jewish believers who went back to a Pharisaic pathway of 'performance religion' in an attempt to gain God's favour, thus moving away from justification through faith in Christ and his merits alone. Whether dressed up in Pagan forms or Jewish forms, Paul describes this mindset as "those weak and miserable principles". This is nothing to do with earnest disciples who gather on the Lord's Day, as the apostles taught them, in the light of the fourth commandment – not to earn salvation, but to rejoice in their salvation by faith in the risen Christ alone.

But what about Colossians 2:16-17?

> *Therefore do not let anyone judge you by what you eat or drink, or with regard to a religious festival, a New Moon celebration or a Sabbath day. These are a shadow of the things that were to come; the reality, however, is found in Christ.*

Surely here is a specific repudiation of Sabbath observance? Well, no. It is unfortunate that both the NIV and ESV translate the Greek as "a Sabbath day". The Greek word is plural, "sabbaths". Nor does Paul say "*the* sabbath," which would be clearly the weekly Sabbath. That word "sabbaths" was used of all sorts of special days set aside in Jewish tradition; it was much broader than merely the weekly Sabbath day. But almost certainly the background here is that Paul is resisting the Judaisers who wanted to see the Colossians revert to all sorts of Jewish practices, including circumcision (2:11-12), and observing the Saturday Jewish Sabbath along with other special days. In the Old Testament these three terms, "festivals, new moons, and Sabbaths", were used together as a phrase to cover the cycle of Jewish religious observances (e.g. 1 Chronicles 23:31, 2 Chronicles 2:4, Isaiah 1:13-14).

The evidence is that many Jewish believers continued to observe the Jewish Saturday Sabbath and *also* met on the Sunday. Paul, however, is determined that the Gentile believers will not be forced to become Jews in order to be acceptable as Christians. That is his great concern at the Council of Jerusalem in Acts 15, as well as when facing the challenge of Judaisers in Colossae, Galatia, and elsewhere. Paul is not rejecting the notion of believers setting apart the Lord's Day to gather in worship, as they did in the early centuries – although most of the believers at that time had to work on Sundays, and therefore met very early in the morning and/or in the evening.[27]

6) The principle that a Sabbath rest remains for believers in the future

Here I am thinking of Hebrews 4:8-11:

> *For if Joshua had given them rest, God would not have spoken later about another day. There remains, then, a Sabbath-rest for the people of God; for anyone who enters God's rest also rests from their works, just as God did from his. Let us, therefore, make every effort to enter that rest, so that no one will fall by following their example of disobedience.*

For some people, the only relevance of the Sabbath principle is as a pointer to the final Sabbath rest in heaven. It has no relevance for us now, only in the future. Clearly the Sabbath principle does take us on to the glories yet to come. The writer of Hebrews speaks in chapter 4:4 of this rest being the rest into which God had entered in Genesis 2. He has already said in v.3 that in Christ by faith, "we who have believed enter that rest." Yet there is something more that lies ahead of us. Thus, saved people as we are, he exhorts us in v.11 "to make every effort to enter that rest," by which he means the climax of salvation that lies beyond this life.

The Sabbath principle found in the first two chapters of the Bible finds its ultimate fulfilment in the Sabbath rest spoken of in the last two chapters of the Bible. That is when finally we enter fully into God's rest of Genesis 2:2-3. We could say that the Sabbath is therefore the overarching principle of the whole Bible. And one day we will be there in Revelation 21 and 22. However, we are not there yet. But every Sunday between now and then is a reminder and a foretaste of heaven, when we are freed from this world's demands and can enjoy God without toil. Piper, again, says:

> *We taste the final rest only in part as we trust in Christ. Therefore the Sabbath principle was not abandoned by the early church. The shadow of Christ across this weary world still offers shade, namely, the first day of the week – the Lord's*

> *day. And the meaning of that day is that Jesus is risen and Jesus is Lord and Jesus is Creator and Jesus is Redeemer and Jesus is the only place of rest for the soul. It's a day for worshipping Jesus. It's a day for saying, by what we do and don't do, that Jesus, not our work and not the money we get from our work, is our treasure and our meaning. It is a special day for the honour and the glory of the Lord. A day for mercy and for man.*[28]

Therefore, in the light of all this, despite all the complexities of the issues, I wish to encourage us to see and rejoice in the abiding relevance of the fourth commandment. God is always wiser than us. He knows we need a day of rest, and we need patterns in our lives which help us give our full attention to spiritual realities. Should we think we know better? Even if people are not Christians, they still benefit from the pattern of a weekly break from work, since that is the way God has designed mankind to function best. Kevin DeYoung's comment is pertinent:

> *God gives us Sabbath as a gift; it is an island of get-to in a sea of have-to. He also offers us Sabbath as a test; it's an opportunity to trust God's work more than my own.*[29]

3. Six Words

What does this mean for our living, our practice, our families, our churches? I would like to leave you with six words.

1) Danger

It is possible to be very focussed on a command in one area, while being blind to disobedience in another. The fourth commandment does not stand alone. We need to take to heart the warning in James 2:10: "Whoever keeps the whole law and yet stumbles at just one point is guilty of breaking it all". Honouring the fourth commandment is just part of a whole-heart, whole-life response to God.

2) Humility

Keep humble and gracious. The Pharisees were zealous to keep the law, as they understood it, but became proud and very harsh and did not share the Saviour's spirit. We must not share their likeness. We have no business to despise our brother or sister in the faith with whom we may disagree on this matter. The true blessing of honouring the fourth commandment is not found in some presumed superior virtue to others, but in a greater likeness and conformity to Jesus. That is what the Lord's Day promotes and encourages. May we all be more like our Lord Jesus who is gentle and humble in heart.

3) Jesus

It is "the Lord's Day". The day is about him, not us. Sunday is not 'me time', it is *his* time. John "on the Lord's Day" heard a voice behind him "like a trumpet", and turned to see who was speaking to him. He saw someone "like a son of man", so awe-inspiring that John fell at his feet as though dead before him. This person said to John, "I am the Living One; I was dead and behold I am alive for ever and ever! And I hold the keys of death and Hades." It is Jesus' Day, the celebration of his victory and his glory. He is to be the centre of this Day. As John Piper writes:

> *Not many people really enjoy what God intended us to enjoy on the sabbath, namely himself. Many professing Christians enjoy sports and television and secular books and magazines and recreation and hobbies and games far more than they enjoy direct interaction with God in His Word or in worship or in reading Christian books.*[30]

Some people claim every day is holy to them; but the danger is that often that can simply mean no day is holy, and Sunday becomes just a day jostling, like every day, with multiple demands and conflicting priorities – shopping, TV, sport, studies, social activities, and, yes, work. The only difference being that we put in church attendance. Let's instead work at making the Lord's Day, the *Lord's* Day – a true holy-day.

4) Best

For some, the outworking of the Lord's Day has been associated with a long list of negatives, restrictions and rules. The Pharisees were the trend-setters for this approach. But I think the true principle is wholly positive. The helpful question is not, "What should I not do?" but, "What is the best thing to do? What will set my heart on Jesus most? How can I best express and reflect his love to others today? How can I enjoy him, his creation, and his people today?" There are many things innocuous in themselves that can be enemies of the best thing. Reflection on this will produce a whole range of answers. Believers will not come up with identical answers, and we should not be judgmental of each other. The great question for us all to ask is: "What is best?"

5) Free

The Lord's Day is Resurrection Day. It is the celebration of Christ risen, of death conquered, of sins atoned for. We are free. We are not yet home, but the victory is totally secure. It is a reminder of Easter Day and of glory ahead. It is a foretaste of heaven. I am free from my normal toils and occupations to enjoy God and his Word, his world, and his people. In a world of rush, rush, rush, I am free to stop and worship and wonder.

I still recall the Sunday the day before the start of important university exams. I woke up with this huge sense of release. I was not going to study that day, and I had a thoroughly good conscience about that. I walked down the corridor, and caught glimpses of my fellow students all stressed out and frantically revising. But I walked along with a bounce in my step. I went off to meet with God's people, to listen to his word, to sing his praises and rejoice in his blessings, as many others have done in their turn. It did me so much good. I was free!

6) Joy

There is a striking testimony from past generations of believers of the joy they found in the Lord's Day. Robert Murray M'Cheyne wrote:

> *A well spent Sabbath we feel to be a day of heaven upon earth. For this reason we wish our Sabbaths to be wholly given to God... We love to rise early on that morning and to sit up late, that we may have a long day with God.*[31]

Thomas Watson wrote:

> *When the falling dust of the world has clogged the wheels of our affections, that they can scarce move towards God, the Sabbath comes, and oils the wheels of our affections, and they move swiftly on. God has appointed the Sabbath for this end. On this day the thoughts rise to heaven, the tongue speaks of God... the eyes drop tears, and the soul burns in love. The heart, which all the week was frozen, on the Sabbath melts with the word... The Sabbath is the market-day of the soul, the cream of time.*[32]

Jonathan Edwards wrote:

> *The Christian Sabbath is one of the most precious enjoyments of the visible church... The Lord Jesus Christ takes delight in his own day: he delights to honour it; he delights to meet with and manifest himself to his disciples on it.*[33]

I fear that when we turn away from honouring the fourth commandment, we pay a high price individually and corporately. These saints speak a language of spiritual joy that the world of British evangelicalism would do well to recover and taste again.

A Very Short Bibliography

Begg, A, *Pathway to Freedom: How God's Law Guides our Lives*, Moody, 2003

Beale, G K, A New Testament Biblical Theology: The Unfolding of the Old Testament in the New, Baker, 2011

Carson, D A (Ed.), *From Sabbath To Lord's Day*, Wipf and Stock, 1999

DeYoung, K, *Crazy Busy*, Crossway, 2013

DeYoung, K, *The 10 Commandments*, Crossway, 2018

Edwards, B, *The Ten Commandments For Today*, Day One Publications, 2002

Frame, J M, *The Doctrine of the Christian Life*, P&R Publishing, 2008

Gaffin, R, *Calvin and the Sabbath*, Mentor, 1998

Gundry, S N (Ed.), *Five Views on Law and Gospel*, Zondervan, 1999

Pipa, J A, *The Lord's Day*, Christian Focus, 1997

John Piper sermons available online at www.desiringgod.org

Schreiner, T R, *Forty Questions About Christians and Biblical Law*, Kregel Academic, 2010

References

1. Carson, D A (Ed.), *From Sabbath To Lord's Day*, Wipf and Stock, 1999
2. Douglas Moo in Gundry, S N (Ed.), *Five Views on Law and Gospel*, Zondervan, 1999, page 88
3. Edwards, B, *The Ten Commandments For Today*, Day One Publications, 2002
4. Pipa, J A, *The Lord's Day*, Christian Focus, 1997
5. Frame, J M, *The Doctrine of the Christian Life*, P&R Publishing, 2008
6. Beale, G K, *A New Testament Biblical Theology: The Unfolding of the Old Testament in the New*, Baker, 2011)
7. DeYoung, K, *Crazy Busy*, Crossway, 2013
8. *Thinking Biblically About Sunday: Space for rest or business as usual?*, Jubilee Centre, 2015, see https://static1.squarespace.com/static/62012941199c974967f-9c4ad/t/620e7eb0325b24272accf129/1645117130683/TBA+Sunday+Short+Guide+-+Jubilee+Centre.pdf as at 26 April 2023
9. Carson, D A (Ed.), *Op cit*, page 17
10. Frame, J M, *Op cit*, page 515
11. *Ibid*, page 572
12. *Ibid*, pages 531-532
13. 'Is There a "Lord's Day"?', John Piper sermon, *Desiring God*, 2 October 2005, see www.desiringgod.org/messages/is-there-a-lord-s-day as at 26 April 2023
14. Schreiner, T R, *40 Questions About Christians and Biblical Law*, Kregel Academic, 2010, pages 215-216
15. Strickland, W G in Gundry, S N (Ed.), *Op cit*, page 82
16. Douglas, J D, *The Illustrated Bible Dictionary: Part 3*, IVP, 1998, page 1355
17. Calvin, J, *Genesis*, Banner Of Truth, 2000, pages 106-107
18. John 7:53-8:11 is absent from most of the earliest manuscripts of the New Testament, however as Don Carson comments: "there is little reason for doubting that the event here described occurred, even if in its written form it did not in the beginning belong to the canonical books". See Carson, D A, *The Gospel According to John*, Apollos, 1991, page 333
19. 'Remember the Sabbath Day to Keep It holy', John Piper sermon, Desiring God, 6 October 1985, see www.desiringgod.org/messages/remember-the-sabbath-day-to-keep-it-holy as at 26 April 2023
20. Frame, J M, *Op cit*, page 556
21. Carson, D A (Ed.), *From Sabbath To Lord's Day, Op cit*, page 65
22. *Ibid*, footnote 54, page 89
23. 'Is the Sabbath Still Required for Christians?', *The Gospel Coalition*, 14 October 2010, see https://www.thegospelcoalition.org/blogs/justin-taylor/schreiner-qa-is-the-sabbath-still-required-for-christians/ as at 26 April 2023
24. Moo, D J in Gundry, S N (Ed.), *Op cit*, page 356
25. Is There a "Lord's Day"?', John Piper sermon, *Desiring God*, 2 October 2005, see www.desiringgod.org/messages/is-there-a-lord-s-day as at 26 April 2023
26. Moo, D J, *The Epistle to the Romans*, Eerdmans, 1996, footnote 74, page 842
27. Acts 20:7 – in his commentary on Acts, John Stott notes: "…it was an evening service or meeting, for if Paul's address ended at midnight, it can hardly have begun at midday! No, it probably began at about sunset, the congregation assembling for worship at the conclusion of their day's work." See Stott, J R W, *The Message of Acts*, IVP, 1990, pages 319-320); Alikin, V A, *The Earliest History of the Christian Gathering: Origin, Development and Content of the Christian Gathering in the First to Third Centuries*, Brill, 2010, pages 40-49 and 79ff (accessed at https://brill.com/display/title/17341 as at 26 April 2023); Pliny the Younger, *Letters*, 10.96
28. 'Is There a "Lord's Day"?', John Piper sermon, *Desiring God*, 2 October 2005, see www.desiringgod.org/messages/is-there-a-lord-s-day as at 26 April 2023
29. DeYoung, K, *Op cit*, pages 91-92
30. 'Remember the Sabbath Day to Keep It holy', John Piper sermon, *Desiring God*, 6 October 1985, see www.desiringgod.org/messages/remember-the-sabbath-day-to-keep-it-holy as at 26 April 2023
31. Bonar, A A, *Memoir and Remains of Robert Murray M'Cheyne*, Banner of Truth, 2004, page 597
32. Watson, T, *The Ten Commandments*, Christian Classics Ethereal Library, pages 87 and 89 (accessed at https://ccel.org/ccel/watson/commandments/commandments as at 26 April 2023)
33. Murray, I H, *Jonathan Edwards: A New Biography*, Banner Of Truth, 1987, page 186